This book belongs to …

Tips for Talking and Reading Together

Stories are an enjoyable and reassuring way of introducing children to new experiences.

Before you read the story:

- Talk about the title and the picture on the cover. Ask your child what they think the story might be about.

- Talk about what a hairdresser does. Has your child ever been to the hairdresser with you?

Read the story with your child. After you have read the story:

- Discuss the Talk About ideas on page 27.

- Talk about the things that you find at the hairdresser on pages 28 – 29 and then find them in the pictures of the story.

- Do the fun activity on page 30.

Have fun!

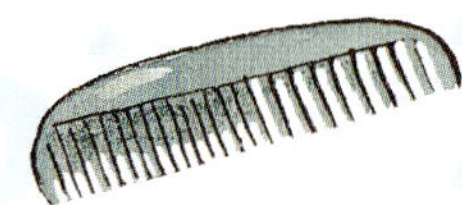

Find the combs hidden in every picture.

Going to the Hairdresser

Written by Roderick Hunt
and Annemarie Young
Illustrated by Alex Brychta

OXFORD
UNIVERSITY PRESS

Mum had some old photos.

"This is me with my family," she said, "when I was a little girl."

Biff looked at the photos. She had an idea. "Let's have
a family photo, and give one to Gran as a surprise!"

"That's a good idea," said Dad.

"Gran would love it. But we need to look smart."

"We should all go to the hairdresser," said Mum.
"Kipper's hair needs cutting and so does Chip's. We'll
all have a trim."

The next day, they all went into town. Chip and Dad stopped at the barber shop.

"We'll see you later," said Dad.

"Come on, Biff and Kipper," said Mum, "we're going to
the hairdresser."

The hairdresser was called Jon.

"Have you brought your teddy in for a fur cut?"
said Jon.

Kipper laughed. He liked Jon.

Jon had a special seat. He put it over the arms
of the chair.

"This is the driving seat," he said. "Climb up and let's go."

"Here's the spray to make your hair wet," said Jon.
"You can try it on Ted."

"And here's the magic gown," said Jon. "This keeps Teddy safe while I cut your hair."

"Keep Ted still," said Jon. "Don't let him escape."

Jon sprayed Kipper's hair and began to cut it.

"Now keep very still," said Jon. "I'm going to cut around your ears."

"It tickles!" said Kipper. He found it hard to keep still, but he did.

"You were very good, Kipper," said Jon.

Kipper was pleased. He looked at Biff. She was having her hair cut too.

The hairdresser was cutting Biff's fringe. Biff had
her eyes shut.

"Put your tongue in," said Kipper, "or you'll get
hairs on it."

Mum was pleased with Biff and Kipper. "You have been good," she said. "We all look much better!"

Dad and Chip came home.

"Oh no!" said Mum.

"We've had new haircuts!" said Dad. "Don't you
like them?"

Dad and Chip had wigs on. They were playing a trick.

"You are funny, Dad," said Biff.

"I have an idea!" said Mum.

The next day, the family went to have the photo taken for Gran.

"You all look very smart," said the photographer.

The photographer made them sit close together.

"Look at the camera," she said. "Smile!"

"Now we want you to take another photo," said Mum.

"My goodness!" said the photographer.

All the family had funny wigs on.

"This will make Gran laugh," said Chip.

"Which picture shall we give Gran first?" asked Biff.

"This one or the proper one?"

"This one, of course," said Mum.

"My goodness!" said Gran, when she saw the funny
picture. "You all need to go to the hairdresser!"

Talk about the story

What do you find at the hairdresser?

Talk about the things you see on this page. Can you think of anything else you might find at the hairdresser?

back mirror

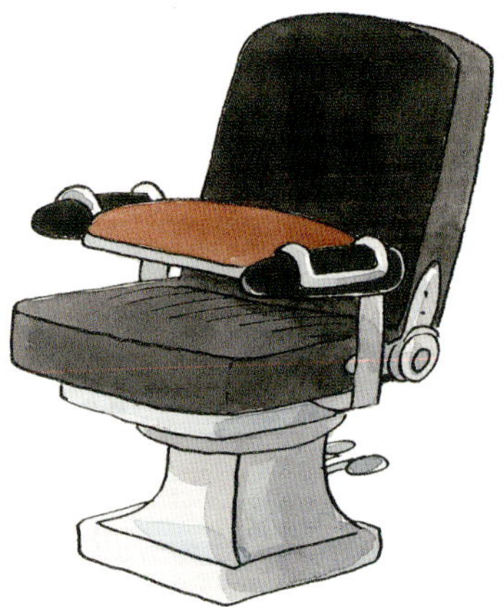

chair with
special seat

combs

water spray

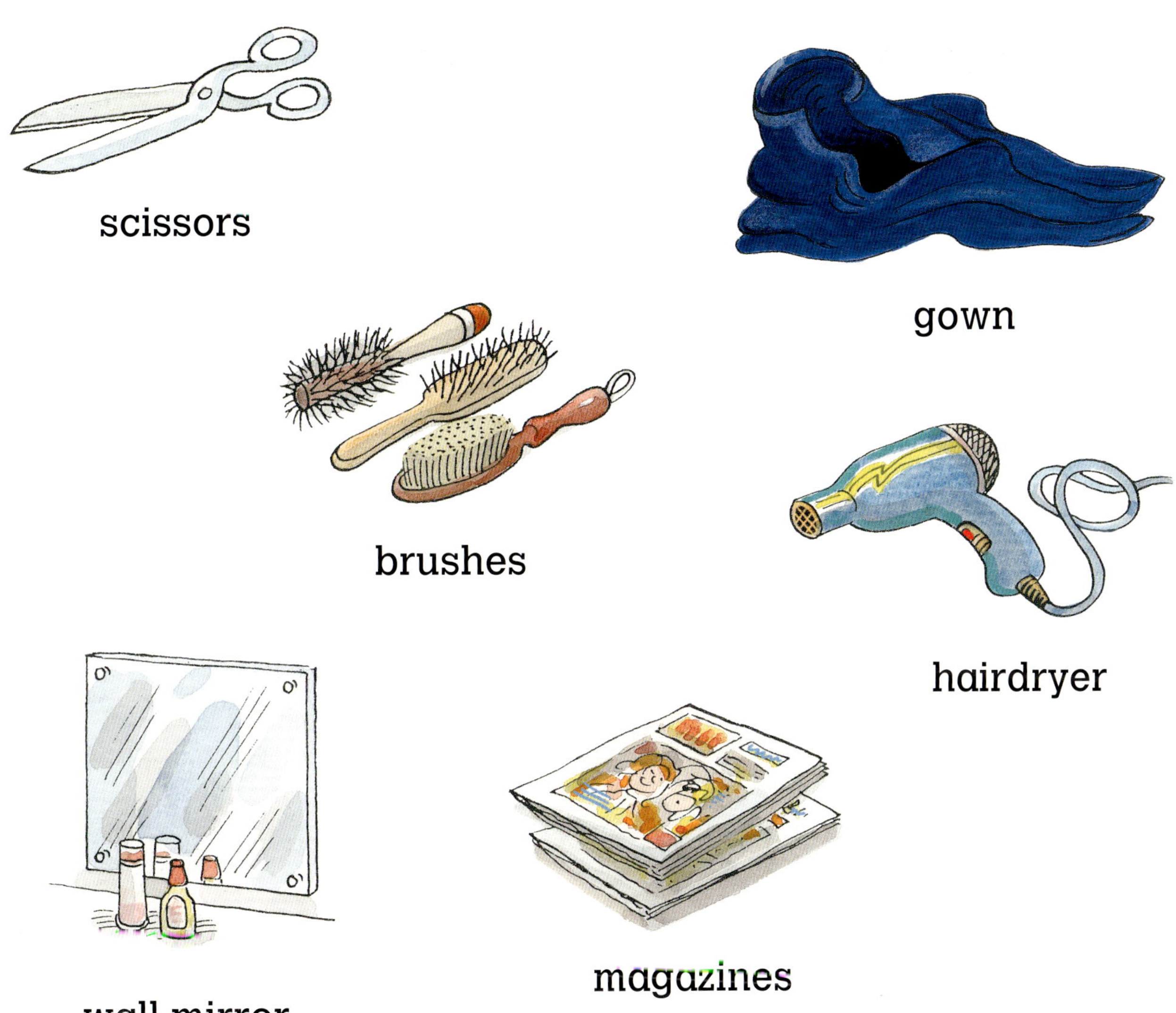

Now look back at the story and find these things
in the pictures.

Spot the difference

Find the five differences in the two pictures of Kipper.

Have you read them all yet?

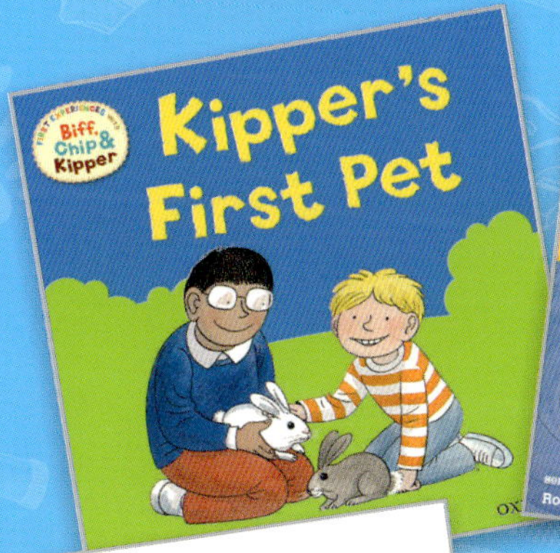

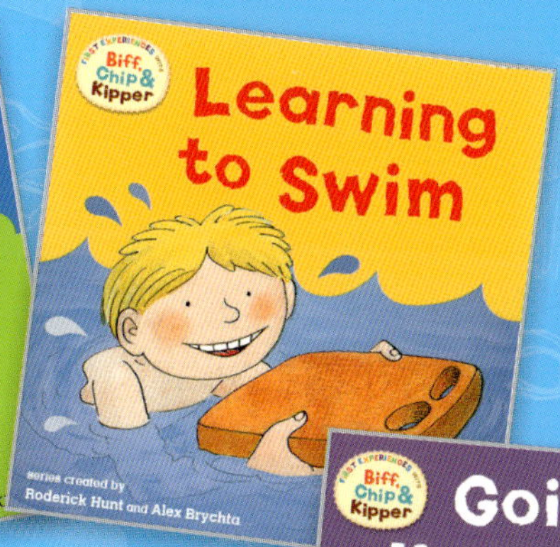

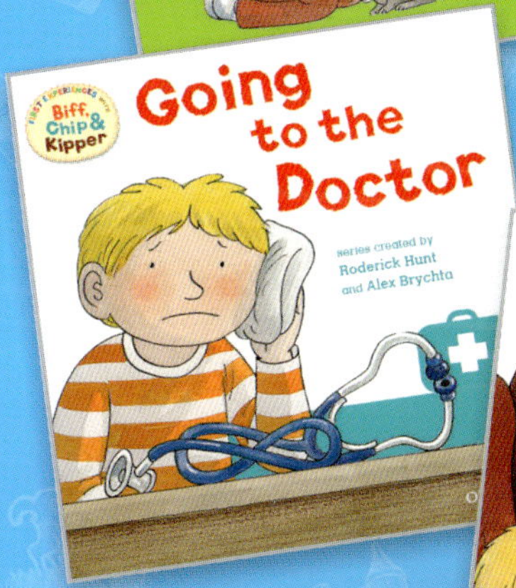

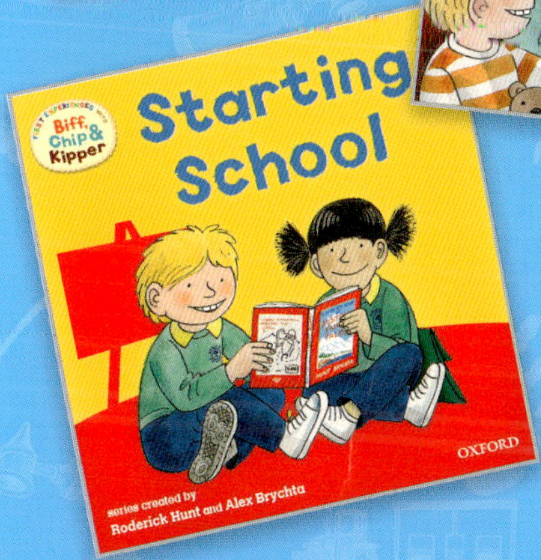

Kipper's First Pet

Learning to Swim

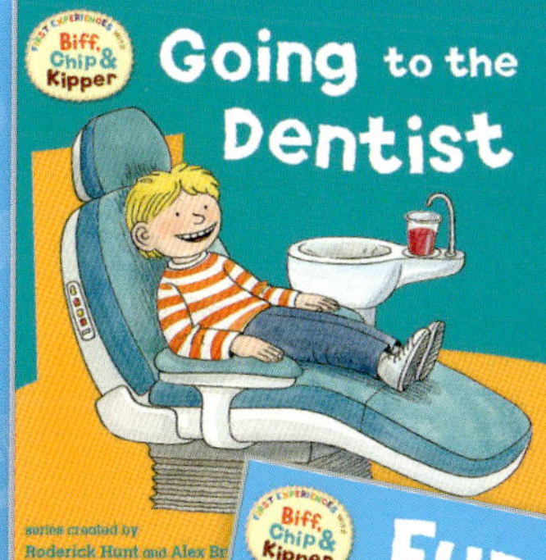

Going to the Doctor

Going to the Hairdresser

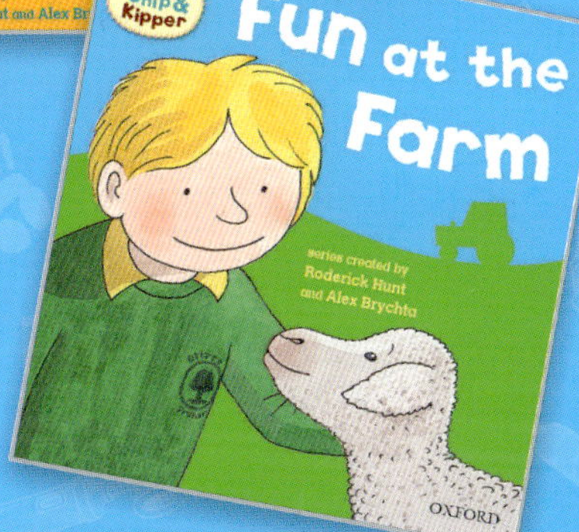

Going on a Plane

Starting School

FIRST EXPERIENCES Flashcards
55 cards

Also available:
- Kipper Gets Nits!
- At the Hospital
- At the Optician
- Bottles, Cans, Plastic Bags
- On a Train
- At the Vet
- At the Match
- At the Dance Class

Read with Biff, Chip and Kipper
The UK's best-selling home reading series

Phonics

First Stories

	Phonics				First Stories			
Level 1 Getting ready to read	 Kipper's Alphabet I Spy	 Chip's Letter Sounds	 Biff's Wonder Words	 Floppy's Fun Phonics	 Get On	 Floppy Did This!	 Up You Go	 Six in a Bed
Level 2 Starting to read	 I am Kipper	 Cat in a Bag	 The Red Hen	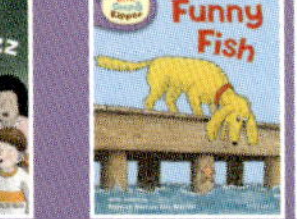 The Fizz-Buzz	 Funny Fish	 Silly Races!	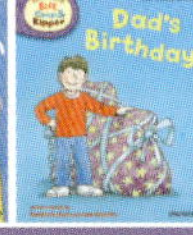 The Snowman	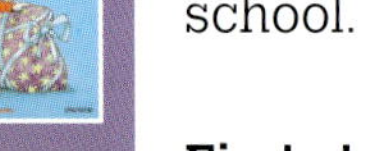 Dad's Birthday
Level 3 Becoming a reader	 Such a Fuss	 Shops	 The Sing Song	 The Backpack	 Poor Old Rabbit	 I Can Trick a Tiger	 Super Dad	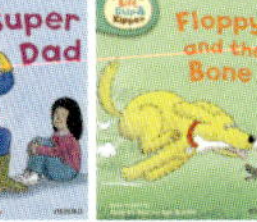 Floppy and the Bone
Level 4 Developing as a reader	 Wet Feet	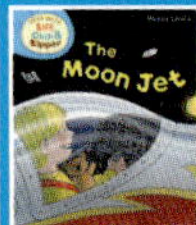 The Moon Jet	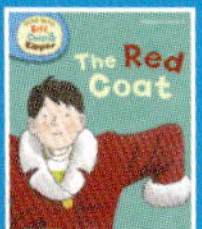 The Red Coat	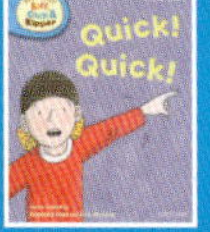 Quick! Quick!	 Missing!	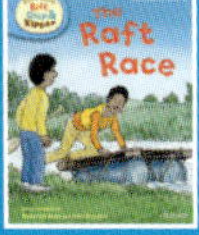 The Raft Race	 Dragon Danger	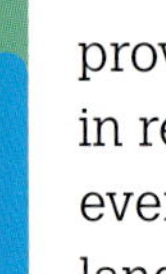 The Spaceship
Level 5 Building confidence in reading	 Egg Fried Rice	 Craig Saves the Day	 Seasick	 Dolphin Rescue	 Hungry Floppy	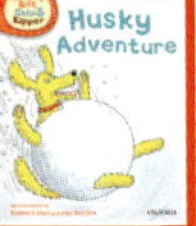 Husky Adventure	 Trapped!	 Looking after Gran
Level 6 Reading with confidence	 Gran's New Blue Shoes	 Ice City	 Save Pudding Wood	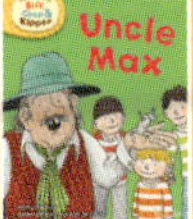 Uncle Max	 Hairy-Scary Monster	 Mountain Rescue	 The Lost Voice	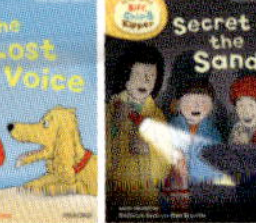 Secret of the Sands

Phonics stories help children practise their sounds and letters, as they learn to do in school.

First stories have been specially written to provide practice in reading everyday language.

OXFORD
UNIVERSITY PRESS

Great Clarendon Street, Oxford OX2 6DP
Text © Roderick Hunt and Annemarie
Young 2007
Illustrations © Alex Brychta 2007
First published 2007
This edition published 2012

10 9 8 7 6 5 4 3 2
Series Editors: Kate Ruttle, Annemarie Young
British Library Cataloguing in Publication Data available
ISBN: 978-0-19-848791-3
Printed in China by Imago
The characters in this work are the original creation of Roderick
Hunt and Alex Brychta who retain copyright in the characters.
With thanks to Suzanne Eden and John Hunt